D0566265

WITHDRAWN

What Do You Know About
The Gold Rush?

PowerKiDS
press™

New York

Lynn George

Published in 2008 by The Rosen Publishing Group, Inc.
29 East 21st Street, New York, NY 10010

Copyright © 2008 by The Rosen Publishing Group, Inc.

All rights reserved. No part of this book may be reproduced in any form without permission in writing from the publisher, except by a reviewer.

First Edition

Editor: Joanne Randolph
Book Design: Kate Laczynski
Photo Researcher: Kate Laczynski

Photo Credits: Cover, p. 1 © Edwin Stocqueler/Getty Images; pp. 5–7 (top), 9 (top), 14, 18–20 © North Wind Archives; pp. 7 (bottom), 9 (bottom), 13, 15–17 © Getty Images; pp. 11, 21 Shutterstock.com.

Library of Congress Cataloging-in-Publication Data

George, Lynn.
  What do you know about the Gold Rush? / Lynn George. — 1st ed.
      p. cm. — (20 questions : history)
  Includes bibliographical references and index.
  ISBN 978-1-4042-4188-6 (library binding)
  1. California—Gold discoveries—Miscellanea—Juvenile literature. 2. Frontier and pioneer life—California—Miscellanea—Juvenile literature. 3. Gold mines and mining—California—History—19th century—Miscellanea—Juvenile literature. 4. California—History—1846–1850—Miscellanea—Juvenile literature. 5. Children's questions and answers. I. Title.
  F865.G28 2008
  979.4'04—dc22

                                        2007031270

Manufactured in the United States of America

Contents

The Gold Rush

Have you ever heard of a gold rush? Do you know what a gold rush is? It is the rush of people to newly discovered goldfields in hopes of getting rich quickly. There have been many gold rushes in history. They have taken place in different countries.

The most famous gold rush in U.S. history was the California gold rush. It began when gold was discovered there in 1848. The first large group of gold hunters arrived in 1849. They were called forty-niners, in honor of the year. The California gold rush changed the United States forever.

Here a man pans for gold in one of California's streams. Though many people came looking, most people did not find a lot of gold.

◆ It was January 24, 1848. James Marshall was in charge of the men building a sawmill for John Sutter. Marshall saw something gleaming in the water. It was gold!

James Marshall was a carpenter and wheelmaker. He traveled west from New Jersey when he was 18.

2. Where in the world is Sutter's Mill?

◆ John Sutter built a farm where the American River meets the Sacramento River, in northern California. The sawmill was on the American River about 50 miles (80 km) northeast of the farm. It was in the **foothills** of mountains, called the Sierra Nevada.

John Sutter was very wealthy and successful until he lost all his land and money during the gold rush.

Sutter's dream was to have a huge farm. Sutter did not want lots of gold hunters coming. He tried to keep Marshall's discovery a secret. Word got out anyway.

This picture shows Sutter's Mill, on the banks of the American River.

7

4. How many people did you say came?

News of Marshall's discovery spread around the world. Thousands rushed to California's goldfields. By 1852, more than 250,000 people had come. That gave California more than two times as many people as it had in 1847!

5. Where are the women and children?

Most gold hunters were men. They left behind their wives and children. The men hoped to get rich quickly and return home. Few did.

People sometimes used all the money they had to travel by boat to America. They hoped to strike it rich in California's goldfields.

6. Where did all these people come from?

Gold hunters came from all over the world. They came from the eastern United States, Mexico, and Canada. They came from South America and Europe. They came from China, Russia, Australia, and Pacific Islands such as Hawaii and Tahiti.

This picture shows the crowded harbor of the mining town of Sacramento. The town was formed in 1848.

7. How far do I have to walk?

Some gold hunters crossed the United States by **covered wagon**. The wagons were so full of belongings that many people walked the whole way. It was over 2,000 miles (3,219 km) and could take six months.

This group is traveling through the Sierra Nevada on their way to California in 1850. The road west was not an easy one, and not everyone made it.

Some people took a ship around the tip of South America. The trip was 15,000 miles (24,140 km) long and took eight months or more. Others took a ship to Panama. Then they made a hard trip through Panama's rain forest and then boarded another ship to California. This trip was about 7,000 miles (11,265 km) long and could take four months or more.

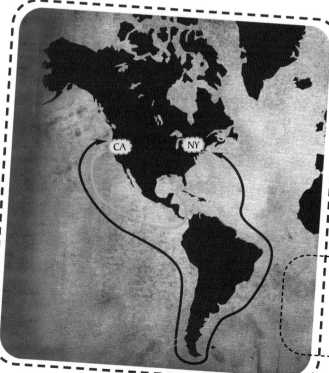

The red line on this map shows the general path boats took around the tip of South America. The orange line shows the way people traveled if they went through Panama.

9. Is that where I am going to live?

Miners commonly lived in camps. Often a miner's house was a tent. Sometimes it was made of cloth fixed to poles. Lucky miners might live in a cabin with several other miners. Sometimes there were simple buildings where miners could rent a room.

Miners often worked 10 or more hours a day. They cooked food over open fires. The lack of fruit and vegetables made some miners sick. Illness and death were common in the camps. Miners made laws for their camps. However, crime was still a problem. Indians, African Americans, and miners from other countries were often treated badly.

This picture shows what a mining camp around 1850 looked like. Some mining camps grew into small towns.

Miners did not have many places to buy the food and supplies they needed. They had to pay whatever the **merchant** wanted to charge. A miner might earn $8 to $10 a day. Bread cost 75 cents. An egg could cost $3. An apple might cost $5. A cooked dinner might cost $25. A pair of boots or a blanket could cost as much as $100!

Here miners weigh their gold at a bank. Some miners were lucky and found enough gold to get by. Others were not as lucky.

There was not much to do for fun in the mining camps. There was also not much time for fun. Miners wrote letters home. They also played card games.

This picture shows miners singing and dancing after a long day of back-breaking work.

12. Is finding gold as easy as they say?

Gold was easy to find at first. It was right on the ground. However, the easy gold was soon gone. Miners worked harder to find less.

13. Did you hear about the latest gold find?

Big gold **mines** were found in the Sierra Nevada foothills north and south of Sutter's Mill. Four were found in the first year.

As gold became harder to find, miners started having to dig into the hills and blast rock to find more.

Panning was a simple **method** based on the fact that gold is heavier than dirt. One person could do it alone. The miner put dirt in a flat pan. He held it in a stream and tipped it to one side a little. He **swirled** it carefully. The water washed away the dirt, leaving behind the gold.

Here men are shown panning for gold. It was simple, but it was still hard work.

All miners hoped to get rich. Some did. One miner found $17,000 in gold in one week. Some brothers working together found $1,500,000 in gold in one year! However, most miners did not get rich. Only about 1 out of 20 miners wound up with more money than he had to start with. The rest were lucky to make enough to get by.

Gold mining was a lot of work, and it was unlikely that the person was going to find any gold. People kept coming to the goldfields anyway.

Samuel Brannan became rich by supplying groceries, tools, land, and alcohol to the miners.

Some people got rich without mining for gold. They were merchants who sold goods to miners. Samuel Brannan was the first to become rich. Levi Strauss **invented** jeans to sell to miners. There were also many others.

17. Where did all the Californian Native Americans go?

There were about 200,000 Native Americans in California in 1848. The gold hunters wanted Indian land. They forced Native Americans off their land or killed them to get it. They made laws that said Native Americans had no rights and it was lawful to kill them. By 1870, there were only about 30,000 Indians left in California.

Native Americans had lived in California for thousands of years. During the gold rush, the new settlers made laws that said Native Americans had no rights and it was lawful to kill them.

California was a U.S. **territory** in 1848. It had about 100,000 Native Americans and 15,000 other people at the time. However, the gold rush brought such huge numbers of people that California was soon ready to become a state. It became the thirty-first state, in 1850.

This is California's state flag. American settlers first raised the bear flag during an uprising against Mexican rule.

19. What happened to the hill that used to be there?

After the easy gold was gone, miners used new methods to find gold. Miners changed the land forever. Huge pipes sprayed water with such force it washed away hills. Machines cut tunnels in mountains. Rocks and dirt filled streams. Toxic **mercury** was used to get gold out of rock. Mercury is still in the soil today.

California became an important state. The country needed a faster way to carry people and goods between California and the eastern United States. Congress finally agreed to build a **transcontinental** railroad. The railroad was finished, in 1869. The West then grew even faster.

20. When does the train arrive?

Glossary

covered wagon (KUH-verd WA-gun) A wagon with a top of heavy cloth that is held up by pieces of wood or metal.

foothills (FUHT-hilz) Hills at the base of a group of mountains.

invented (in-VENT-ed) Made something new.

merchant (MER-chunt) Someone who owns a business that sells goods.

mercury (MER-kyuh-ree) A toxic, silver-colored element.

method (METH-id) A way or system.

miners (MYN-erz) People who hunt for valued stones or dig for them in the earth.

mines (MYNZ) Pits, underground tunnels, or other places from which stones are taken.

swirled (SWURLD) Caused something, such as water, to move in a spinning motion.

territory (TER-uh-tor-ee) Land that is controlled by a person or a group of people.

transcontinental (trants-kon-tuh-NEN-tul) Going across a continent. A continent is one of Earth's seven large landmasses.

Index

Web Sites

Due to the changing nature of Internet links, PowerKids Press has developed an online list of Web sites related to the subject of this book. This site is updated regularly. Please use this link to access the list:
www.powerkidslinks.com/20his/grush/